Logos
Identity by design
217 Delta Street, Toronto, Ontario M8W 4E7
Telephone (416) 251-7365

Designing Corporate Symbols

This book is dedicated to A.T. (Tom) Turnbull, a great teacher.

Designing
Corporate
Symbols

David E. Carter

ART DIRECTION *BOOK* COMPANY

19 West 44th Street
New York, New York 10036

First Printing, January 1975
Second Printing, March 1976
Third Printing, December 1976
Fourth Printing, February 1978

Published by **Art Direction Book Company,** 19 West 44th Street,
New York, New York 10036   212 / 986-4930

Library of Congress Catalog Card Number: 74-29013

International Standard Book Number: 0-910158-32-0

List of Symbols

11. Action Associates Agency
12. Advertising Designers, Inc.
13. Air Comfort, Inc.
14. Airport Marina Hotels
15. Alberto Culver, VO5
16. ABC Radio Networks
17. ABC Television
18. American Security Bank
19. Amtrak
20. Anneberg Gallery
21. Applied Power Inc.
22. Armour
23. Atlanta Galleria
24. BPC Industries
25. Bakers Best
26. Barkow Petroleum
27. Bauer & Black
28. Bioscience Laboratories
29. Boise Cascade
30. Book of Life
31. Braniff Educational Systems
32. Braniff Place
33. Brookline Electric
34. Bruce, Robert
35. Buffalo Braves
36. California Casualty Ins. Cos.
37. Canteen Corporation
38. Century Products
39. Children's Medical Relief International
40. City Investing
41. Club de Pesca
42. Cluster Quart System
43. Colonial First National Bank
44. Community Renewal Society
45. Condominium at John Hancock
46. Consolidated Foods Corp.
47. Consumer Alliance
48. Continental Auction Company
49. Cornnuts Inc.
50. Corporate Identities Division
51. Cotton Incorporated
52. Crown Zellerbach
53. Derhomannesian, Armen
54. Devin Food Equipment
55. Dry Creek Lodge
56. Dunkin' Donuts
57. Dyna Structures Inc.
58. Eaton Corporation
59. Eighth & Diamond Street Gang
60. Electrovision Productions
61. Elgin Watch Company
62. Environmental Measurements
63. Financial Utility Organization
64. Foulds Macaroni
65. Ben Franklin Stores
66. Franklin Typographers
67. Gould, Inc.
68. T.J. Grant Realtors
69. Growth Fund of America
70. Gulf Contracting Incorporated
71. HARP
72. Hawaiian Air
73. Hunt Manufacturing Co.
74. Illumination Industries Inc.
75. Indian Lakes Estates
76. Ironwood Country Club
77. Kaptain Klean Dry Cleaners
78. Keystone International, Inc.
79. Kimberly-Clark Corporation

80. Jack Klassen
81. L.A. Ventures
82. LaFontaine
83. Logan Tower
84. Machine Tool Exchange
85. Manhattan School of Music
86. "Manson"
87. Marcona Corporation
88. MIT, alumni gathering
89. Martin Senour Paints
90. Medical Data & Financial Corp.
91. Herman Miller
92. Modine Mfg. Co., 1-R Radiators
93. Monique Montgomery Knitwear
94. Motorola
95. National Bank of Washington
96. National First Corporation
97. North American Squash Racquets
98. Ooma II
99. PM Water Beds
100. Packaging Corporation of America
101. Pants o/off!
102. Peace Corps
103. Peoples Trust and Savings Bank
104. Perfection American
105. Philadelphia Flyers
106. Photographix
107. Polaris Enterprises, Inc.
108. Quality Real Estate Investments
109. RCA Corporation
110. Randcard Division, Rand McNally
111. Rand McNally/York Ltd.
112. Realize Ecology
113. Redbird Industrial Park
114. RiverView
115. San Francisco Racquet Club
116. Service Concepts
117. Sierracin Corporation
118. Spectra-Physics, Inc.
119. Storkline Furniture
120. The Summit

121. Superior Metalworking Systems
122. Sutro & Co. Incorporated
123. Synthane-Taylor Corporation
124. Technicolor
125. Teledyne
126. Teradyne
127. Texas Real Estate News
128. Timberwine
129. Total Financial Services
130. USEMCO Inc.
131. USA
132. USIA
133. USIA
134. Unifinity Foundation
135. Uniforms Unlimited, Inc.
136. United Engineers
137. Vaughn Walls, Inc.
138. Vantage Planning Systems
139. The Vault
140. Vista
141. WMAL
142. Western Mutual Insurance
143. Western Ventures
144. Westlake Moving & Storage
145. White Birch Lakes
146. Wingers Erection Company
147. Yosemite National Park
148. Young Musicians Foundation

A good corporate symbol doesn't just appear from nowhere. More often than not, a great deal of time, thought, and research go into the successful design.

A good symbol accurately portrays the personality and function of the company. For every good corporate mark, there is a story behind it.

In the preparation of this book, a number of top graphic designers and design firms were asked to "submit your very best work, and tell, in your own words, why the mark was designed as it is."

This book is the result of that compilation. The marks and their descriptions contained herein should be of great value to the designer of symbols, to corporate decision-makers, and to design students.

Action Associates Agency is a firm comprised of specially trained people who plan insurance programs for insurance companies and commercial firms.

Its trade mark suggests what it does, the pinpointing of an insurance problem (dot) and the solving of that problem by direct, personal (arrow, man). The forming of the letter A as a paper shelter further emphasizes the importance of the agency.

It appears embossed and in black and white.

Designer: Thomas A. Rigsby
T. Rigsby, Design
West Los Angeles, California

Advertising Designers, Inc., a graphic design office. Designing the letter forms for "AD" was relatively easy, but they needed to be put in an unusual but appropriate context. Finally, while erasing an outlined version of the mark, we found just what we were looking for. The end result was achieved by die-cutting the "AD" and making a rubbing from it.

Designer: Carl Seltzer
Advertising Designers, Inc.
Los Angeles, California

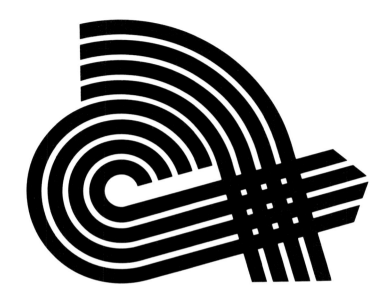

Air Comfort Inc. is a mechanical contracting firm dealing basically in industrial and commercial heating and air conditioning systems. Keeping this in mind, we have taken an "A" and a "C" and combined them into a mark which while both elements are able to be seen comes across as an "A." The multi-line effect along with the directional arrow was used to denote the air flow interaction which takes place in a total air conditioning and heating system.

Colors are orange and brown; these were colors which were already in use by Air Comfort and because of the equity which they seemed to have in them, they were retained.

Designer: Jim Hernandez
Miller/Hernandez Design Consultants
Atlanta, Georgia

Airport Marina Hotels, a chain of hotels operated by Fred Harvey, Inc., are located in park-like, waterside settings near the major airports in San Francisco, Los Angeles, Dallas and Albuquerque. The mark — which is used in signing as well as advertising and collateral material — symbolizes the concept of flight and the hotel's waterside location.

Designer: Primo Angeli
San Francisco, California

Alberto Culver, an important producer of hair care products and beauty aids, has adopted this symbol to reflect strong, positive assurance of quality in a product line that has grown year after year. When shown in color, the VO is often white reversed out of a dark background, and the entire inside V area is then colored. The panel containing a reverse underlined 5 matches that color.

Designer: Dickens Design Group
Chicago, Illinois

American Broadcasting Companies, Inc.
American Contemporary Radio Network

American Broadcasting Companies, Inc.
American FM Radio Network

American Broadcasting Companies, Inc.
American Information Radio Network

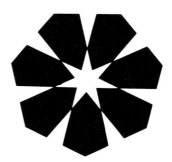

American Broadcasting Companies, Inc.
American Entertainment Radio Network

These symbols as a group and individually have since 1967 represented the four ABC Radio Networks. (1) The American Entertainment Radio Network is symbolized by a radiating star, appropriate to its format of general music and guest star entertainment. (2) The gathering and disseminating of news and information is the idea behind the positive and negative, in-and-out arrows of the American Information Radio Network symbol. (3) The American Contemporary Radio Network symbol is presented as an activity of eccentric circles appearing to move within each other representing this network's contemporary music format. (4) The classic simplicity of symphonic musical elements expresses the American FM Radio Network.

Designer: G. Dean Smith
San Francisco, California

In constant and consistent use since 1962, this communicative symbol has represented the American Broadcasting Company's five owned and operated stations: WABC-TV, New York; KABC, Los Angeles; KGO-TV, San Francisco; WLS-TV, Chicago; and WXYZ-TV,. Detroit. The importance of informing the viewer of the channel number was the major consideration resulting in the use of the numeral "7" (each of the five stations is Channel 7 in its area). However, the aesthetics of both positive and negative spaces in relation to the figurative form were of equal design importance in the final development of this symbol.

Designer: G. Dean Smith
San Francisco, California

American Security Bank of Honolulu, Hawaii, is represented by this mark. The direct usage of the national bird rising from the securely locked letters, A and S, suggests the firm name; moreover, this combination implies the national strength and trust desired in a financial institution.

It usually appears in solid black.

Designer: Thomas A. Rigsby
TriArts, Inc.
Los Angeles, California

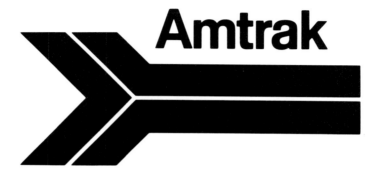

The name Amtrak was developed by Lippincott & Margulies for this country's first nationwide rail passenger service. The letters *Am* signify the American orientation linked with *trak* to provide the transportation posture. The colors of red, white and blue, of course, enhanced the American orientation. The symbol itself in the form of a stylized arrow signifies speed and purpose of direction.

Designer: Lippincott & Margulies, Inc.
New York City

The Anneberg Gallery is a small art/craft gallery in San Francisco. The mark is a particular "equilateral" version of the Moebius Twist. This form was primarily chosen as the gallery mark for its enigmatic quality, a concept often expressed in the works which hang in a gallery. Where possible, it is used in dark warm grey on white.

Designer: Harry Murphy & Friends
San Francisco, California

Applied Power Inc. adopted this housemark to denote their auto-
motive aftermarket and fluid power products worldwide. The symbol
was designed to be forceful and unique. It is a combination of an
early hex shape trademark owned by the company for hydraulic tools,
and the engineering force arrow pointing to upper right quadrant. The
outward and upper movement symbolizes the application of power to
move machinery or goods — the capability of "Applied Power."

Designer: Charles MacMurray Design Inc.
Chicago, Illinois

The new Armour symbol and logotype purposely retain established equities of the traditional Armour Star trademark, while simultaneously conveying an image of a truly contemporary corporate entity. Highly distinctive and easily recognizable, the new communications program was designed not only to create a total family look for Armour packaging, but also for application to the corporation's entire range of visual expressions.

In order to create sales appeal among female customers, the system is specially designed to generate a good product look and also make a strong statement on product quality.

Designer: Walter Landor Associates
San Francisco, California

Atlanta Galleria

Atlanta Galleria is a Total Environmental Complex, consisting of basically commercial, residential, and recreational facilities.

The elements of the symbol are a lower case A and a lower case G, which when combined convey the feeling of a Galleria; the loose definition of which is, a corridor with a central light source.

The colors are olive green and yellow. The green represents the complete natural surroundings of the Galleria and the yellow has the connotation of being the central light source.

Designer: Charles Nemon/Jim Hernandez
Miller/Hernandez Design Consultants
Atlanta, Georgia

Trademark for a desk accessory and signage manufacturer: BPC Industries, Hoboken, New Jersey.

This company, previously known as Bank Products Corporation, made accessories for banks; however, management decided to branch out to all areas of desk accessories, and to incorporate architectural signage in their activities. Since a name change eliminating the word "bank" was in order, the client decided upon BPC Industries.

The designers chose the most logical and direct approach; utilizing the "BPC" initials and engineering one typographic device to become each of the three letters depending upon which way it is turned. This epitomizes BPC's flexibility in servicing its architectural clientele which appreciates these modular characteristics. The mark is used on all material, and works well in grids, patterns and repeats.

Designers: Appelbaum & Curtis
New York, N.Y.

Bakers Best was a mark developed in conjunction with a packaging program for the Royal Cake Co., Winston-Salem, North Carolina. The symbol is obviously a baker with his rolling pin. It was styled very graphically to promote an up-dated image that the packaging program would eventually follow. The symbol is contrasted not only within itself with sharp and curvilinear forms but also the typography used reverted back to the good old days to give stability and further contrast.

Colors: White/Dark Brown/Ochre/Pink . . .White was used for the baker's hat and shirt as it was to denote freshness. The basic outlined form of the baker was utilized in dark brown for proper contrast and because it also has a connotation of the outer crust of most baked products. The hand and face of the baker were pink purely for separation purposes and the rolling pin was ochre.

Designer: Jim Hernandez
     Miller/Hernandez Design Consultants
     Atlanta, Georgia

Barkow Petroleum: The approach used in this mark was to visually express the company's three main operations: the blending, packaging and distribution of oil products. The mark itself symbolizes a drop of liquid (oil) surrounded by or "packaged in" the letter "b" as well as the concept of blending and movement. The mark is dynamic in a design sense, and visually describes the company's activities.

Designer: Primo Angeli
San Francisco, California

Bauer & Black sells elastic goods for health care, supports everywhere on the human body. The basic design was intended to emphasize their special knit and flexibility. Support under tension and movement was the theme. It is applied to all packaging forms.

Designer:　Goldsholl Associates
　　　　　　　Northfield, Illinois

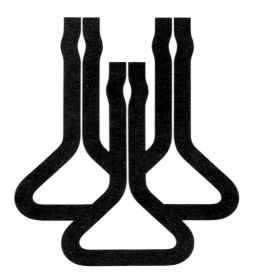

Bioscience Laboratories is a three-division service lab which works with medical offices throughout the world. The company needed visual continuity in its advertising and collateral material. At first the idea of three interlocking flasks seemed trite, but once it was simplified and expressed graphically the concept proved to be a sound one. The mark has been a flexible and effective tool for Bioscience Labs.

Designer: Primo Angeli
San Francisco, California

The Boise Cascade symbol was designed in 1963. Its concept was based on an up and coming, growing corporation of diversified interests, as symbolized by the arrow forms shaping upward growth. Though the company's origin was in forest products, the containing circle was intended to represent both a continuum of its diversified interests and a containment symbolizing stability.

Designer: G. Dean Smith
San Francisco, California

The Book of Life is a religious encyclopedia based upon the Bible. The symbol is an open book overlayed with a cross. The branches of the cross are further embellished with leaf shapes to suggest growth.

Designer: Robert Vogele
             RVI Corporation
             Chicago, Illinois

Braniff Educational Systems, Inc. is a training school for Braniff International. It teaches flight engineers, ground operations personnel, A&P mechanics, and reservations and ticket personnel.

The primary intention was to symbolize the training of people while maintaining a symbol with flexibility in a variety of applications. Also, we desired for this symbol to be consistent with other Braniff International designs.

The design symbolizes a student, listening to the instructor from behind his desk. The use of a human figure completes the intent to symbolize the training of people.

Designer: David Harper
             Unigraphics, Inc.
             Dallas, Texas

BRANIFF PLACE

Braniff Place is a resort hotel located off Padre Island on the Texas Gulf Coast. It is managed by Braniff International Hotels.

This design intends primarily to complement the surrounding area in association with the pleasing, warm atmosphere of Braniff professional management. The gull is symbolic of the sea as well as flight. It prints in warm colors on a sand paper stock.

Designer: Don Day
Unigraphics, Inc.
Dallas, Texas

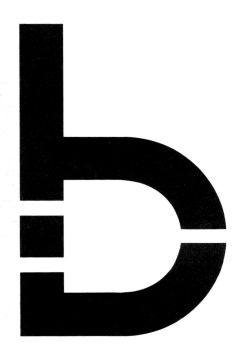

Brookline Electric is an electrical contractor working in the San Francisco area. A large percentage of Brookline's business was found to be composed of small, residential projects. The mark is simply the letterform "b" in which the counter or negative space is an electrical plug. Conceptually, the unique thing about this is that, while Brookline's work has almost nothing whatever to do with electrical "plugs" per se, the residential consumer, who is the promotional target of the mark, visualizes electrical work quite readily in terms of a "plug" because of his or her everyday familiarity with household appliances. The mark is used in "electric blue" on a white background whenever possible.

Designer: Harry Murphy & Friends
San Francisco, California

Robert Bruce is a long-time manufacturer of mens' and boys' knit-wear.

Our intention was to create a strong masculine mark to function as a ski mark in winter and a sun mark in summer, with the color varying for the season and the promotion. The stencil letter was designed to enhance and strengthen the identity.

Designer: Kramer, Miller, Lomden, Glassman/Graphic Design
Philadelphia, Pennsylvania

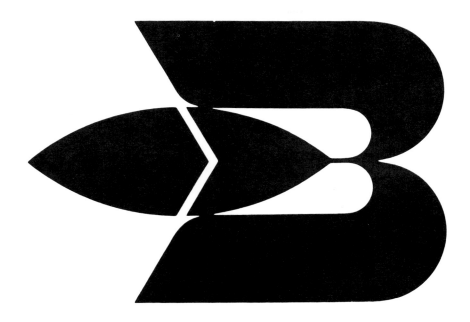

Buffalo Braves is an expansion entry in the National Basketball Association. The symbol was designed for instant recognition and multi-use. The B in black; the tip of the feather in red.

Designer: Mel Richman, Inc.
Bala-Cynwyd, Pennsylvania

California Casualty Insurance Companies. This growing organization consisting of diverse insurance specialists companies decided in 1969 to unify and modernize their corporate identification, previously based on a line etching of Yosemite's El Capitan. The symbol is based on the letters "C," with a torch- or flame-like interpretation to symbolize warmth, friendliness, growth and classical solidity. Varying colors within a golden earth tone range have been utilized to represent the various companies within this insurance group.

Designer: G. Dean Smith
            San Francisco, California

Canteen Corporation (a subsidiary of Trans World Airlines, Inc.) is one of the country's major specialists providing food and vending services to business, industry, institutions, fine restaurants and private clubs and sports stadium concessionaires. The abstract element of the symbol is blue and black plus the firm name in blue (underlined in black) denote the blending of food, service and people into a total marketing image — a food vending service.

Designer: Dickens Design Group
Chicago, Illinois

Based in San Jose, California, Century Products manufactures and distributes a complete line of "ecology oriented" detergent products. They are sold door-to-door in much the same manner as the well-known Avon line. The mark actually consists of three images: a group of "bird forms" symbolizing clean air; a group of "tree forms" symbolizing clean land; and a group of "drop forms" symbolizing clean water. In fact, the corporate image for Century Products employs all three marks, used both together and individually. In packaging, for example, each package uses one part of the three-part mark, and since they are always personally shown door-to-door, they always appear as a group on packages. This allows all three visual images to be used in a larger size for greater impact, and at the same time be viewed essentially together, by the consumer at the point of sale. The "birds" are blue, "drops" are blue-green, and the "trees" are green. All three colors are the same value and closely analagous.

Designer: Harry Murphy & Friends
San Francisco, California

Symbol for a medical care organization: Children's Medical Relief International, New York and Vietnam.

Extremely simple symbol was designed to be recognizable under the extreme conditions of hazard in the Vietnam war zone, where a major hospital is set up to provide plastic and reconstructive surgery for the child casualties of the war. Flame symbolizes the words of Adlai Stevenson describing Eleanor Roosevelt, "She would rather light a candle than curse the darkness."

Symbol is designed for essential, rapid recognition on architecture, vehicles, and especially on uniforms and armbands where its reproduction must be achieved even under primitive conditions.

Since Children's Medical Relief International cares for children of both North and South Vietnam, this is a symbol that is known and respected by all combatants.

Designers: Appelbaum & Curtis
New York, N.Y.

While there is an abstraction of the initial "C" and even one of the initial "I," it was not the main objective of the symbol. Rather, we have here a structural shape which creates a varying optical illusion of dimension in this mark for City Investing.

Designer: Robert Miles Runyan & Associates
Los Angeles, California

Club de Pesca is a resort hotel located in Acapulco, Mexico, owned and managed by Braniff International Hotels. Club de Pesca in Spanish means "fishing club." This hotel in Acapulco has long been noted for the Sailfish caught from its boats.

The Club de Pesca symbol was updated with the intention of giving the reader the excitement of catching one of these beautiful fish. Club de Pesca prints in a sea-blue, and the sailfish is an aqua-green.

Designer: Jack Evans
Unigraphics, Inc.
Dallas, Texas

This mark was designed for Mead Packaging's Cluster Quart System; a wrap-around style of packaging which encloses three quart bottles within its outer shell. The symbol therefore denotes these qualities as described. The "Qt." being the abbreviation for quart is the main segment of the mark, and the three dots were used to represent the three bottles that the packaging system houses within itself.

Colors are blue and magenta. The blue was used for the strength it relates to the package structural system and magenta because it could be related to one of the many flavored beverages which might be carried in this type of package.

Designer: Jim Hernandez
Miller/Hernandez Design Consultants
Atlanta, Georgia

The eagle which is used on currency and is also a symbol used in conjunction with the Colonial period is stylized to form a symbol that denotes strength and solidity that customers require from a bank. Very appropriate for Colonial First National Bank.

Designer:　Corporate Identities Division
　　　　　　Gray & Rogers, Inc.
　　　　　　Philadelphia, Pennsylvania

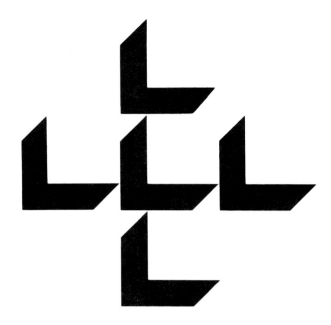

The descriptive copy line used with the symbol of the Community Renewal Society of Chicago is "renewing the city through faith in action."

The mark is a cross composed of four cubes defined by the shadow or black area. The three-dimension aspect of the mark is to suggest buildings of the city.

The Community Renewal Society is a private religious organization that works to bring better understanding and economic advancement to inner city residents.

Designer: Joseph Sparkman
RVI Corporation
Chicago, Illinois

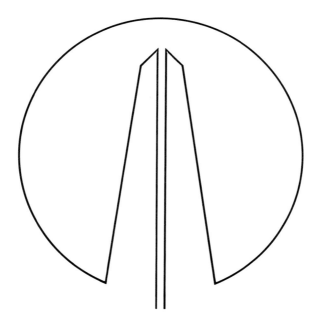

The Condominium at John Hancock Center. The John Hancock Center is a well-known Chicago landmark. Once the decision was made to convert the apartment condominiums, the task of doing a symbol for the sales program was primarily a matter of isolating the strong visual characteristics of the building and refining them into a usable combination of shapes. The burden of the mark was to communicate quickly, in a variety of applications, throughout an extensive sales program. A line version of the familiar silhouette, within a circle, gave us a mark capable of conveying both the strength and the elegance of The Condominium at John Hancock Center.

Designer: Joe Hutchcroft
RVI Corporation
Chicago, Illinois

46

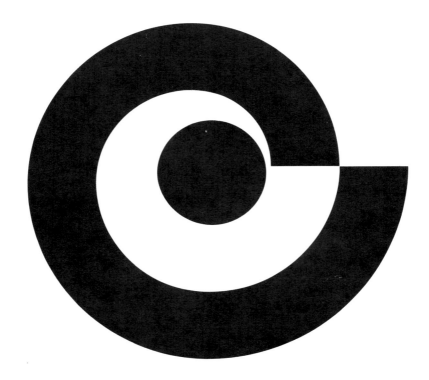

Consolidated Foods Corporation is composed of more than 128 companies operating in a wide array of product and service areas. As a result, management needed a communications system that would be applicable to each individual company, as well as create a strong identity for the parent company.

The stylized "C" combined with the logotype is an unusual, memorable marketing signature which provides a feeling of strength and movement — two core attributes of this major corporation.

Designer: Walter Landor Associates
San Francisco, California

Solidity and interchange are the two major characteristics of Consumer Alliance, an action oriented group since 1971 concerned with the continuous exchange of ideas and actions to create more powerful influence as a unified body in the area of consumer affairs. These ideas have been expressed through the continuity of a Moebius loop structure, triangulation for strength and a semblance of the letter "A."

Designer: G. Dean Smith
San Francisco, California

48

Continental Auction Company. The client desired two elements incorporated into a new symbol: (1) the initials of the company, and (2) a "national" symbol, preferably a star, to denote the nationwide aspects of the company. Factors considered in the design included individuality, an up-to-date appearance, and above all, simplicity, as it was to be utilized in many sizes, on a variety of surfaces, and in black and white as well as color.

Designer: Steve Connatser
Unigraphics, Inc.
Dallas, Texas

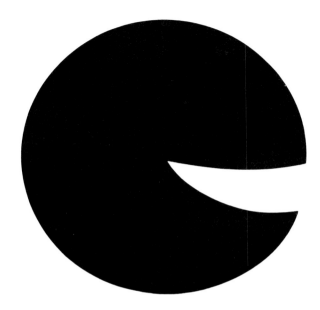

In 1936, Albert F. Holloway founded a company based on a toasted, salted snack product made of corn, and until 1962, the company was known as Olin Manufacturing Company, though the product was packaged under the name of Cornnuts. When corporate management passed to the next family generation, a corporate identification program seemed in order and it was decided to adopt Cornnuts Inc. as the new corporate name, with new symbolism, packaging and an entirely fresh corporate "face" — thus a derivation, a smiling face, from the letter "C," and the crunching good taste of Cornnuts symbolized for all.

Designer: G. Dean Smith
San Francisco, California

The letters C and I combined to form a strong graphic symbol for a firm that designs symbols — Corporate Identities Division.

Designer: Corporate Identities Division
Gray & Rogers, Inc.
Philadelphia, Pennsylvania

Bringing the cotton industry's image up-to-date, Cotton Incorporated's symbolism concentrates on the natural qualities of the product and the well-known shape of the cotton boll. The rectangular form enclosing the symbol and logotype was designed to accommodate consumer information messages and specific promotions.

The color scheme of white and brown further emphasizes the "natural wonder" of cotton, as well as providing visual versatility for an industry dealing in hundreds of colors and products.

Designer: Walter Landor Associates
            San Francisco, California

The Crown Zellerbach symbol is another example of abstracted company initials. The letters "C" and "Z" are formed by the white lines bisecting the black shape. It works as well in black and white as it does in color. When the symbol is used in the orange and red corporate colors, the "C" shape is orange separated by the diagonal white line from the red "Z" shape.

Another symbolic element present in the Crown Zellerbach mark is the abstract form of a roll of paper on a press. And paper is their business. Motion dynamics are quite strong in this symbol.

Designer: Robert Miles Runyan & Associates
Los Angeles, California

Symbol for Armen Derhomannesian, landscape architect and city planner. The symbol combines organic and structural elements into one unit, as does the architect.

Designer: Robert Cipriani
Gunn Associates
Boston, Massachusetts

Trademark for a restaurant and commissary supply company; Devin Food Equipment, Columbus, New Jersey.

This "knife, fork and spoon" design is a shorthand symbol for all food equipment. Devin is the largest of this type of firm in the east. Additionally, these extrusion-like shapes structure a "d" which stands for Devin.

This utensil-like symbol is on all Devin material; such as the stationery and forms, the headquarters building, packaging, ads and tractor-trailers. The accompanying name is in poster blue and the "knife, fork and spoon" symbol itself is in an appropriate silver color.

Designer: Joel Mitnick
Appelbaum & Curtis
New York, N.Y.

The Dry Creek Lodge is located at the very beginning of the Wind River foothills in western Wyoming. It offers wilderness experienced from a luxurious base. Its trips are both unique and sophisticated; its design, decor and identity are the same. The undulating lines usually appear in blue and green.

Designer: Jennifer Gritton
The Design Partnership/Bruce Beck Associates
Evanston, Illinois

Trademark for a food franchise firm: Dunkin' Donuts of America, Randolph, Massachusetts.

This firm wished to change its old symbol of a man made of donuts and crullers because it was being confused in the customer's mind with another similar firm: Mr. Donuts. In addition, the man's figure was difficult to discern by motorists on the highway, where most of their franchise shops are located.

Also, a cup of coffee was added pictorally to the finished symbol, since the Dunkin' Donuts management felt that, in their business, it was a necessary compliment to donuts. Both the donut and coffee cup are juxtaposed to suggest a coffee-and-donut snack in the quickest terms. The client's records prove that the symbol has been a particularly successful part of their sales program.

Symbol in pink and rasberry is on architecture, cups, napkins, take-out packaging, uniforms, and all ancillary elements.

Designer: Appelbaum & Curtis
New York, N.Y.

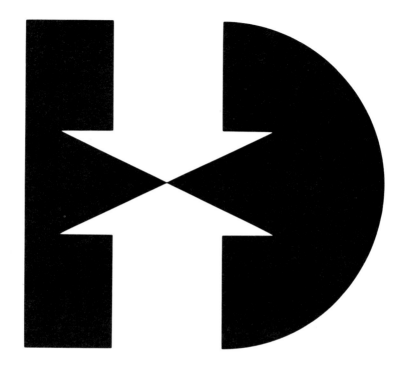

Dyna Structures Inc. is a coordinated group of space physicists and structural space engineers.

Their work deals with the design of space frames and ground stations. The mark was created to graphically indicate the ground to space tensions. To increase the retention value, the mark is used in black only.

Designer: Kramer, Miller, Lomden, Glassman/Graphic Design
Philadelphia, Pennsylvania

In order to simplify and strengthen its identity, Eaton Corporation shortened its name from Eaton, Yale & Towne, Inc. The single name was then rendered in a precise but unique juxtaposition of its five blue letters which forms the keystone element of its identification system. The company is a $2 billion diversified corporation engaged in the manufacture of automotive and truck components, materials handling equipment, power transmission, control and security systems.

Designer: Lippincott & Margulies, Inc.
New York City

The Eighth & Diamond Street Gang is a neighborhood gang of boys in a depressed area of Philadelphia.

The Greater Philadelphia Movement under the direction of William Wilcox, now Deputy Director of Social Affairs for the state of Pennsylvania, asked for our counsel in developing an identification, easily retained, good gang acceptance and easily duplicated. A first step toward giving corporate dignity to the rough and tumble organization.

Designer: Kramer, Miller, Lomden, Glassman/Graphic Design
Philadelphia, Pennsylvania

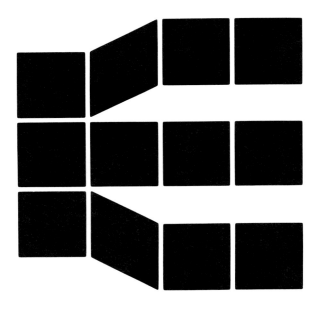

Electrovision Productions established the first of several permanent film, slide and three-dimensional multi-media audiovisual presentations in 1970. The symbol, based on the letter "E," was structured to imply both multi-usage and three-dimensional effects.

Designer: G. Dean Smith
San Francisco, California

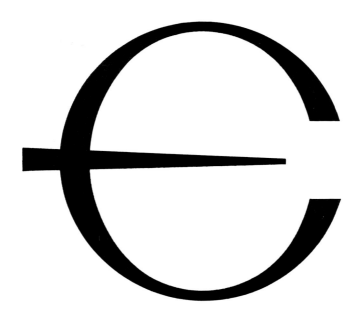

The trademark for the Elgin Watch Company (Elgin National) was based upon a semi-circular watch dial face. Even the crossbar of the "E" recalls a watch hand. The mark forms an "E" of classic proportions suitable for product or print applications. The softness of the form and the variance of the oval stroke relate well to the jewelry market.

An unusual requirement in this assignment was the ability of the trademark to reduce cleanly in watch dial faces in sizes as small as 1/16 of an inch.

Designer: Charles MacMurray Design Inc.
Chicago, Illinois

Environmental Measurements has been involved since 1969 with measurement and precise data on pollution, extending to many dimensions and cycles of nature. The just-touching points of the arrows within the circle of the symbol are intended to symbolize the extremely fine and precise measurements taken by this company. The circle and directions of the bars reflect the company's major expertise in accurate calculation of pollutants, land to air and air to land.

Designer: G. Dean Smith
San Francisco, California

Recognizing the reliable identity verification potential of speech, in 1974 the Financial Utility Organization developed a system that provides instantaneous speaker recognition through computer systems, with initial use in financial transactions. Much like a fingerprint, speech exhibits particular, unique characteristics. The symbol has been designed as a representation of such a "voice print," containing movement that is electronic in feeling yet still organic in nature.

Designer: G. Dean Smith
San Francisco, California

64

Foulds Macaroni had no trademark. We were commissioned to design the packaging. A symbol was needed and we offered to design one. The letter F was created from a bound sheaf of wheat which bent in the wind.

Designer: Goldsholl Associates
            Northfield, Illinois

Ben Franklin Stores needed a new symbol. We designed the mark using four basic elements. Ben Franklin used a key (1) in flying his kite to test the electricity which sparked (2) in a thunder storm. The heart (3) represented the friendliness of the local store and the letter F (4) finalized the design.

Designer: Goldsholl Associates
            Northfield, Illinois

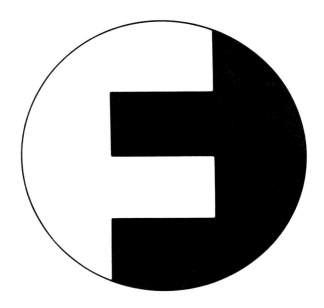

Franklin Typographers is a good, honest, full service type shop, without frills or corporate ostentation. Their mark reflects that unembellished directness. The interlocking "F" form relates well to the bare metal type and the ink impression made from it, as well as the negative/positive aspects of film type. Since it reads the same upside down (and indeed, even on its side, the "F" is unmistakable) the recognition value is constant and stable.

I resisted the temptation to use the literal square shape of a type stick and opted for the more esthetic and emphatic circular form. It works equally well as a slug line at the bottom of a type proof (3/16") and as a 6" die-cut delivery label. Its dimension adaptivity is good. It was designed and approved in twenty minutes. I wish all my work was that easy and that effective.

Designer: Richard Hess Inc.
                New York City

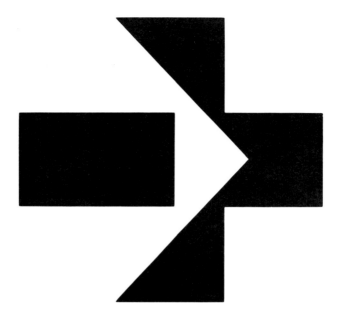

The merger of Gould Inc., primarily a battery manufacturer, with a large engine parts company in 1967, created the need for a visual style to solidify the merger, to set up a system for aligning the numerous segments of the multi-product, multi-national organization, and to assist in raising the new corporation to a more sophisticated marketing position with its main thrust in the electrical and electronic fields. The new trademark visually combines the "positive" and "negative" signs, basic elements associated with the electric-electronic fields, and an arrow connoting the forward thrust of the company. A complete corporate identity system was adopted along with the new mark.

Designer: Peter Teubner
RVI Corporation
Chicago, Illinois

T.J. Grant Realtors sells houses, and uses a strong identity approach to its real estate signs, its advertising and its printed matter.

Designer: Jennifer Gritton
            The Design Partnership/Bruce Beck Associates
            Evanston, Illinois

The Growth Fund of America, a mutual fund which seeks growth of capital. The letters "G" and "F" are designed to create a plant-bud form. This organic shape suggests growth.

Designer: Carl Seltzer
Advertising Designers, Inc.
Los Angeles, California

Gulf Contracting Incorporated is a general contracting company in Sarasota, Florida that was purchased by two young individuals who wanted to change the old image of the company to reflect the new management.

They desired a letter-mark that read "G," "C," "I," and reflected the fact that they built high-rise structures. We felt that this letter-mark solved the problem with an obvious GCI, and a feeling of a high-rise structure being created by the 3-D appearance of the "I."

Colors are olive green, yellow and orange.

Designer: Robert Miller
Miller/Hernandez Design Consultants
Atlanta, Georgia

HARP is the acronym for *H*yaline Membrane *A*ssociation for *R*espra-tory *P*roblems and is the support group for fund-raising for a research and treatment center for this disease which attacks infants.

In developing a recognizable symbol for an acronym, which is in itself a symbol, I try to find a letter which can define what the letters alone cannot tell. In this case, the *A* becomes a safety-pin which sugg-ests infants. HARP therefore relates to babies.

Designer: Gerry Rosentswieg
The Graphics Studio
Los Angeles, California

Built upon a distinctive image and unique physical environment, Hawaiian Air's new identification system projects what Hawaii represents to consumers — fun, excitement, escape. Bold colors, flight sweeps on aircraft and promotional materials, and a new symbol combine to capture the spirit of the islands.

The system's core is the symbol — dubbed "Pualani," or Flower of the Sky by the airline — composed of an island girl superimposed on Hawaii's state flower, the Hibiscus. The colorful graphics effectively evoke Hawaii's sand, surf and lush, tropical foilage.

Designer: Walter Landor Associates
San Francisco, California

Hunt Manufacturing Co. manufactures and distributes the Speedball artist inks and pens.

The symbol conveys the broad stroke of one of their pens with a graphic interpretation of the pen itself in the lower portion of the "S." It could be printed in any color since Speedball inks come in a wide range of colors.

Designer: Mel Richman, Inc.
                     Bala-Cynwyd, Pennsylvania

Illumination Industries Inc. manufactures high intensity light sources. The three "i"'s are the company's initials but also symbolize the light and energy contained within a well defined space. The goal was to express energy, control and organization in a simple graphic statement.

Designer: Primo Angeli
San Francisco, California

An Indian head with stylized trees as the feathered headdress to symbolize the greenery being preserved in the land development are the main elements of Indian Lakes Estates. The bottom part of the mark depicts the water of the lakes in the area.

Designer: Corporate Identities Division
Gray & Rogers, Inc.
Philadelphia, Pennsylvania

Ironwood Country Club, a residential and recreational resort con-
ceived by Arnold Palmer in 1970, is located on a plateau overlooking
Palm Desert, California. With concern for the conservation of nature
and this desert environment, the symbol is designed to reflect the
form of the Desert Ironwood, a tree typical of the desert in which the
resort is located.

Designer: G. Dean Smith
San Francisco, California

Kaptain Klean Dry Cleaners is a small chain of retail service shops in Northern California. The main design concept was to relate a fresh, fun place of business that suggested a spit-and-polish attitude to their unique service. The military aspect was not considered in its current sense, but rather the design evokes a nostalgic relationship to the past. All of this happens within a strong symbol of the cleaner industry — the clothes hanger.

Designer: Robert Pease
Robert Pease & Company
San Francisco, California

Keystone International, Inc., a planned four-seasons resort community, situated in the Rocky Mountains of Colorado, is a wholly-owned and managed subsidiary of Ralston Purina Company. Designed in 1974, this symbol is based on a seven-pointed star that radiates into what can be construed, depending upon usage, to be a snowflake, a flower, a sunburst — with its active dynamism indicating a multiplicity of recreational and learning activities. The structure of the symbol is comprised of the multiple use of the letter "K."

Designer: G. Dean Smith
San Francisco, California

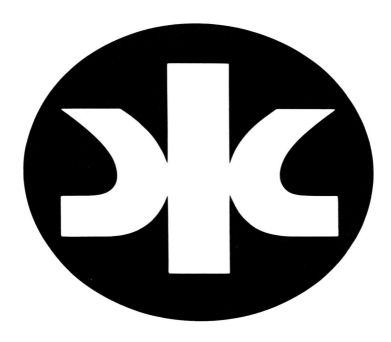

Kimberly-Clark Corporation is a leading producer of trademarked consumer goods with additional interest in forest products, newsprint and fine papers. This symbol was designed to combine their initials, "K-C," in the form of a growth pattern or tree, from which their basic raw materials are derived, and by which the company has been able to expand into correlated product lines.

A worldwide "trademark search" disclosed that the only symbol at all similar to this was a character in the Chinese written language which means "Product of Clear Water." Quite appropriate. When used in color, the mark is rendered in turqouise blue on a horizontal black oval.

Designer: Dickens Design Group
Chicago, Illinois

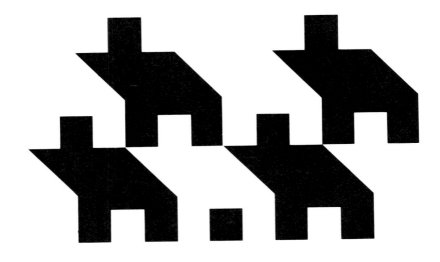

Jack Klassen is a building contractor in San Francisco. I selected the "house form" because it seemed to be an almost archetypal communication about "buildings" or "building." Grouping the house forms enlarges the communication about the size and scope of the projects handled by the contractor. Finally, the "image to ground" relationship becomes visually dynamic because of a polarity shift (black to white to black . . .etc.) This dynamic and visually exciting relationship seems certain to add to viewer involvement and retention.

Designer: Harry Murphy & Friends
San Francisco, California

    L.A. Ventures is the parent company of several other diversified real estate based companies: L.A. Properties, L.A. Management, etc. Keeping this in mind, a mark with the following qualities was developed. A system was utilized to allow one mark to function for all of the various segmented companies. The mark was also designed to show the centrality and the multiplicity of the company. The basic make-up of the mark is a combination of an "L" and an "A."

    The colors are two shades of brown, the dark brown is always applied to the bottom center L.A.; all the rest are in the lighter shade to represent the centrality of the parent company, L.A. Ventures.

Designer: Jim Hernandez
              Miller/Hernandez Design Consultants
              Atlanta, Georgia

Logo for an apartment condominium featuring a giant fountain at the main entrance.

Designer: Dave Lizotte,
Gunn Associates
Boston, Massachusetts

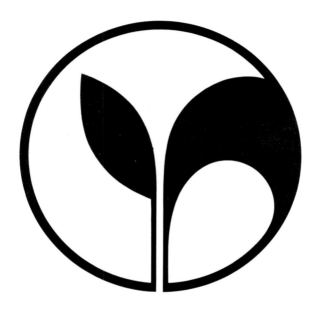

In the Logan Tower logo, the leaf is green, and the tower of water is blue. The green leaf symbolizes the trees in the parklike setting, and the tower of water gets its origin from the water fountain which is a landmark at the Logan Circle, site of a hotel and condominium that was never built.

Designer:　Corporate Identities Division
　　　　　　Gray & Rogers, Inc.
　　　　　　Philadelphia, Pennsylvania

Machine Tool Exchange is a Southern California based company which imports and distributes metal working tools, such as precision milling machines and heavy drilling equipment.

The logo tries to exemplify the strength inherent in this type of equipment. An attempt was made to show a stylized piece of heavy machinery, with the center point of the "M" representing a diamond-like drill bit. Orange has been used with black to add visual force and color.

Designer: Bob Mendoza
Los Angeles, California

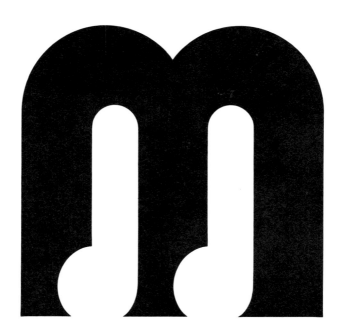

Symbol for a music school: Manhattan School of Music. The strong "M" initial is composed of two characteristics which represent this school of advanced, college-level, musical instruction. First, the arches that form the "M" itself are reminiscent of traditional academia; and second, the negative spaces subtly display one of the standard symbols of music — the half-note.

The symbol is usually displayed in the school's color, ultramarine blue; and it also maintains a bold appearance when seen in black in newspaper advertising.

Designers: Appelbaum & Curtis
New York, N.Y.

"Manson" is a documentary film from American International Pictures. It depicts in vivid detail the career of convicted, hippie, mass murderer, Charles Manson.

The approach to this mark is one of abstract character to suggest the hippie appearance and homicidal personality of Charles Manson. Since the purpose is short range sales promotion, it must get immediate public attention and is important only in inviting the viewer to read further.

In newspapers, it is used at the bottom of ads with a heavy, black border adjoining the sides and enclosing the upper elements.

Designer: Thomas A. Rigsby
T. Rigsby, Design
West Los Angeles, California

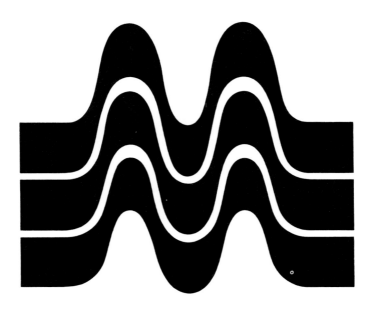

Marcona Corporation is a diversified company involved with many industries. The design problem defined two distinct operations of the firm. The mark had to be used for the mining Division in Peru (the colors are earth tones). In addition, the minerals are transported on their own ships — sea-going tankers (the colors are tones of blue). For Corporate use, the colors were combined. All this is one trademark.

Designer: Robert Pease
Robert Pease & Company
San Francisco, California

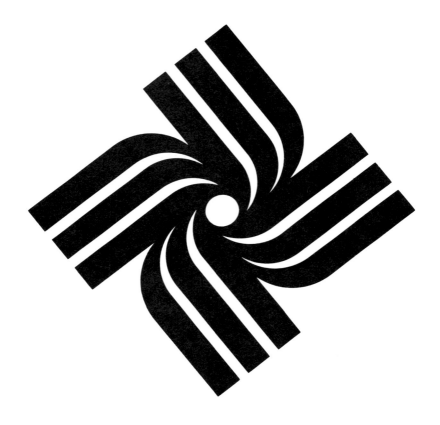

Symbol for an alumni gathering at the Massachusetts Institute of Technology (M.I.T.). The symbol is based on movement and convergence from the four directions of the compass to a central place. The pinwheel feeling adds a note indicative of a festive occasion.

Designer: Robert Cipriani
Gunn Associates
Boston, Massachusetts

Martin Senour Paints. The brush trademark relates to an orderly system of mixing custom colors, the chipping and samplings of these colors and the need to say "Color in the Brush" on all literature and displays. Needless to say, the dots in the bristles were all printed in various related colors.

Designer: Goldsholl Associates
Northfield, Illinois

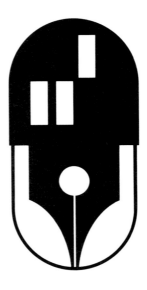

Medical Data & Financial Corporation, a company that specializes in increasing the efficiency, profitability, and liquidity of individual doctors and medical clinics. They help manage a practice by preparing and mailing invoices and statements, collecting delinquent accounts, training clerical employees, completing insurance claims, providing loans against accounts, keeping clients current as to the financial condition of their practice, and assisting in preparation of income tax statements.

They find out what is needed and wanted by doctors to make their practice more profitable and less troublesome. They add their know-how in computer technique, and financial management. They also add a large measure of people-to-people communications.

The symbol is comprised of the key punch form representing the use of computers, a pen point for accounting and personal involvement combined in a capsule representing the medical profession and symbolic of restoration to health.

Designer: Dennis S. Juett
Los Angeles, California

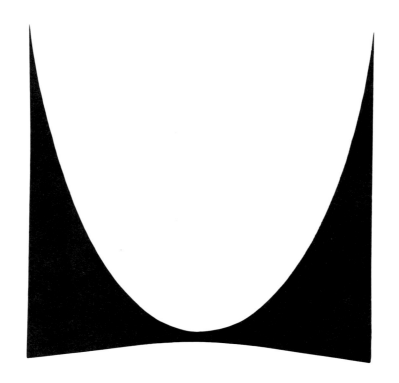

The Herman Miller mark reproduced for the furniture manufacturer in Zeeland, Michigan, is an old mark and apparently very durable. It was done around 1947 and is still going strong. It began as a simulation as a plywood cutout and some of the original applications showed wood grainings on them. Since then it is intended to be used as a flat symbol in red, usually, and despite the many changes in the company over a long period, it remains in active use.

Designer: George Nelson & Company
New York, N.Y.

Designed for product molds and product plates, the brandmark for "1-R" Radiators (Modine Manufacturing Company) offered a rare opportunity to combine the arabic numeral "1" and the capital letter "R" in one unit. The viewer first percieves a capital "R" or a numeral "1" with an additional figure; upon a second glance, the combination is perceived and remembered — far better than two separate configurations.

The numeral-letter form was selected to be appropriate to the crisp metal product — bold but simple.

Designer: Charles MacMurray Design Inc.
Chicago, Illinois

Monique Montgomery Knitwear manufactures custom knitwear.
This mark as monogram was designed to suggest threads of yarn.
Also vieing for a share of the designer clothes market, the client
wanted the mark to act as a designer signature to be applied in
pattern to other products.

Designer: Gerry Rosentswieg
            The Graphics Studio
            Los Angeles, California

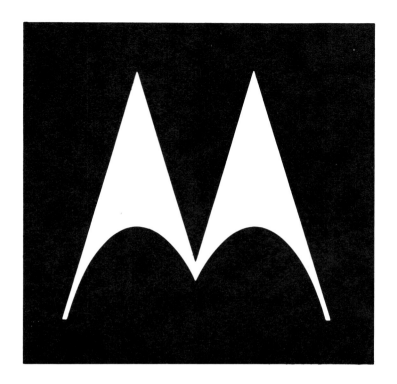

MOTOROLA

The Motorola trademark was designed using two types of sine waves, the curved and angular forms, offering handsome contrasts to each other. It is used on all nameplates, packaging, corporate signage and literature.

Designer: Goldsholl Associates
Northfield, Illinois

The National Bank of Washington. One of the problems facing this venerable bank was that in its marketing territory (District of Columbia) there were two other banks with the word National and Washington in their titles. To help differentiate The National Bank of Washington from these similar banks, a typographic approach was first used to emphasize "Bank of Washington" and de-emphasize "The National," the idea being to get across that this is *the* Bank of Washington. At the same time, a stylized W was developed to help differentiate The National Bank of Washington from its competitors. There are those who also see within this symbol the clenched fist of black power. Considering that much of NBW's marketing territory is heavily black, it engendered a very positive response to this corporate stance.

Designer: Lippincott & Margulies, Inc.
New York City

National First Corporation, a California-based mortgage and real estate company. The "N" with the "1" inside it is about the simplest form this mark could take. The negative-positive quality of the mark makes it unique.

Designer: Detlef Hallerbach
             Advertising Designers, Inc.
             Los Angeles, California

North American Squash Racquets Corp. This mark was recently designed for a holding company that is now building squash racquets courts throughout the East. Our objective was to design a symbol that would convey the product in its environment. The left side of the "swish" is red, the right side is blue; the racquet strings are red and the squash ball is blue. The symbol is contemporary, outstandingly so in a rather reserved sport, recognizable and memorable. That's what it's all about.

Designer: Mel Richman, Inc.
Bala-Cynwyd, Pennsylvania

Ooma II

The sun, the water and the palm trees integrated into a graphic symbol to symbolize a land development in the Hawaiian Islands.

Designer: Corporate Identities Division
Gray & Rogers, Inc.
Philadelphia, Pennsylvania

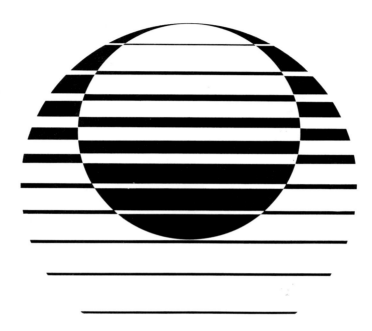

PM Water Beds is a retail store selling and manufacturing flotation furniture. The design concept strived to symbolize and relate the name within its design. The sun rising and setting — days into night. Sleep.

Designer: James St. Clair and Robert Pease
Robert Pease & Company
San Francisco, California

Packaging Corporation of America's symbol reflects the total packaging (or full-service) facilities, including raw material, container fabrication, printing, etc., which the company can provide for its customers. Black "P" on white background encircling a blue dot represents the all-encompassing packaging operations of the firm and is simultaneously indicative of package forming and printing operations.

Designer: Dickens Design Group
             Chicago, Illinois

Pants %off!

"Pants o/off!" is a discount pants store in San Francisco, selling marked-down pants to a young (15-35) customer profile. The store name is appropriately daring, when qualified by the per cent mark in the logo, which clarifies the meaning. The logo is also visually accompanied by the verbal message, "The Discount Pants Store," which further emphasizes the "on sale" idea. Lastly, the logo usually appears in "Sale" red.

Designer: Harry Murphy & Friends
San Francisco, California

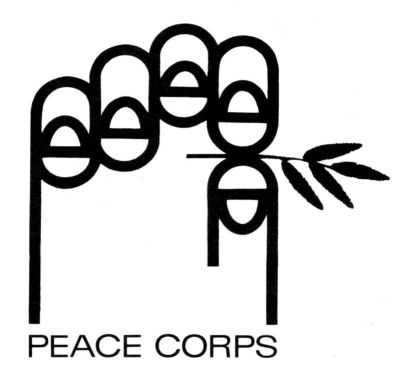

PEACE CORPS

The Peace Corps mark was designed to symbolize the willing hands of all the volunteers holding a stylized olive branch.

Designer: Goldsholl Associates
            Northfield, Illinois

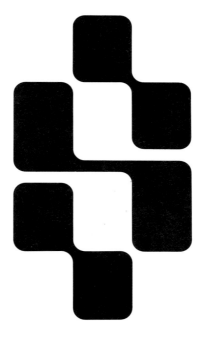

The mark for the Peoples Trust and Savings Bank in Fort Wayne, Indiana was designed to meet the need for a great variety of sizes and applications. For example, it has been built as illuminated sculpture with the illuminated faces matching the black symbol on either side, at the entrances to a number of the bank's suburban offices. Its ancestry should be obvious: the dollar sign. Originally we intended to have it printed in green. Since then a considerable variety of colors have been applied when used on checks, advertising brochures, billboards and newspaper advertising, mailers, annual reports, etc.

Designer: George Nelson & Company
            New York, N.Y.

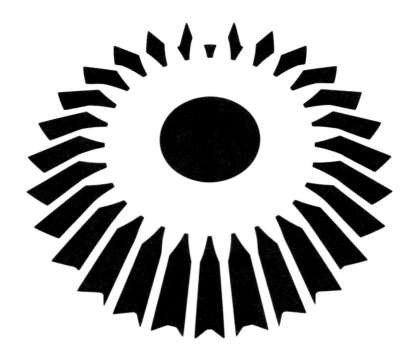

PERFECTION AMERICAN

Perfection American is a stock gear company. Our objective was to design a totally new kind of gear symbol, unlike the thousands of flat, two-dimensional projections commonly seen. The need for a single-color mark was obvious. The mark is applied to all packaging and graphics material.

Designer: Goldsholl Associates
Northfield, Illinois

The Philadelphia Flyers, a team in the National Hockey League. The symbol was designed to convey "who the client is and what they do."

The simplicity and strength of the mark is what we believe has been the success and total acceptance. In one self-contained symbol, it conveys Philadelphia, Flyers, and puck. The colors used were black for the stylized P, and orange for the puck.

Designer: Mel Richman, Inc.
                    Bala-Cynwyd, Pennsylvania

Photographix is a photographic service with capabilities in various styles and approaches to photography and print-making techniques. The camera look-and-feel were incorporated into the logotype for obvious reasons. The mark is used at all angles in printing indicating the action and versatility of the photographers.

Designer: Don Day
Unigraphics, Inc.
Dallas, Texas

Polaris Enterprises, Inc., a manufacturer of charcoal, adopted a symbol designed to say, "all you do is light it." This symbol illustrates the ease of obtaining gourmet-type cooking results by using this product. Reflected are such features as self-starting and quicker cooking. Colors used are white "gloves of quality" with warm red and magenta flames set against a charcoal black background.

Designer: Dickens Design Group
               Chicago, Illinois

Quality Real Estate Investments, a company created to locate and present unique real estate opportunities to a few qualified potential buyers. The concept was to develop an image of quality and a feeling that the company has been in existence for sixty years or so. The trademark was designed with the quality characteristic of a steel die engraving in a style reminiscent of the turn of the century. Once the company is firmly established in the market place, it will be franchised throughout the United States.

Designer: Dennis S. Juett, Don Weller, Jack Hermsen
Los Angeles, California

A bold, simple redesign of the three initials highlighted the change of corporate name from Radio Corporation of America to RCA Corporation. Since it is primarily an innovative, highly sophisticated, technological producer of electronic systems and equipment the posture of the company was re-oriented to reflect these characteristics in all communications by means of nomenclature changes, format, red color, typography, etc. It was applied to signage, vehicles, exhibits, stationery and business forms as well as all advertising and sales promotion material.

Designer: Lippincott & Margulies, Inc.
New York City

The bank credit card system of the Randcard Division of Rand McNally & Company offers both security and access with the card itself being the key to both. The symbol suggests that it is more than a lock.

Designer: Larry Creter
The Design Partnership/Bruce Beck Associates
Evanston, Illinois

Rand McNally/York Ltd. is an English affiliate of Rand McNally
& Company that deals almost entirely in supplying European Airlines
with tickets and other printed forms.

Designer: James Knippen
            The Design Partnership/Bruce Beck Associates
            Evanston, Illinois

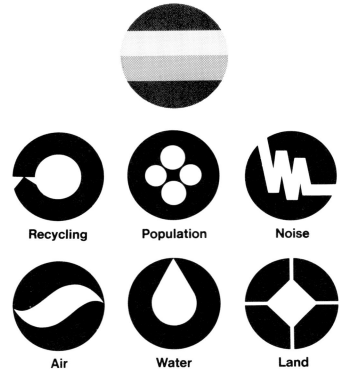

Realize Ecology was organized in 1970 with the goal of disseminating a series of symbols that utilize international graphic standards of symbolism in an effort to increase man's awareness of the necessity of conservation. The earth symbol has been seen by many to represent the elements of sky, water, the surface of the earth and the core of the earth. In color, the symbol progresses top to bottom from a dark blue stripe, to a lighter blue, to a light green and a dark green.

The six sub-symbols were designed as action symbols for specific areas of environmental concern and are implemented utilizing the single color, International Reflex Blue.

Designer: G. Dean Smith
San Francisco, California

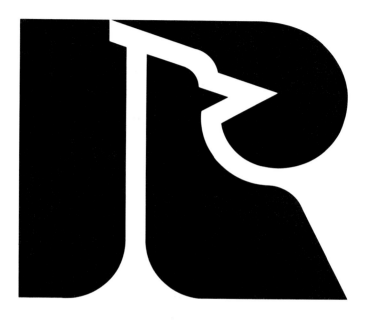

The Redbird Industrial Park mark was designed to add a clean, simple identity to the office park complex by the use of the color red and the image of the bird. The massive "R" (that includes these elements) gives the feel of the construction of the complex itself, as well as a splash of color and appeal to enhance the visual impression of the office complex, and improve its appearance.

Designer: Don Day
Unigraphics, Inc.
Dallas, Texas

RiverView is an adult residential community in the well known wine country of Sonoma County in California. The project mark is the picnic basket shown, and, when used promotionally, the mark is always accompanied by the verbal message "Life is a Picnic at RiverView." Sale of homes in RiverView was promoted with the emphasis on the variety of available outdoor activities for senior citizens. The mark is used in five colors: brown for the "basket," orange and red orange for the round "fruit" shapes, dark olive green for the "bottle," and yellow green for the square "napkin." As a final touch, an actual picnic basket, similar to the mark, (with cloth napkins, a bottle of local wine, etc.) is given to each home buyer at the closing of the sale.

Designer: Harry Murphy & Friends
San Francisco, California

The San Francisco Racquet Club is a private tennis complex in downtown San Francisco. The concept was to symbolize the city, its Golden Gate Bridge and tennis itself. If you really see and study a tennis ball, one can almost see the division within its shape. The companion color, naturally, is green — for tennis courts.

Designer: Robert Pease
Robert Pease & Company
San Francisco, California

Service Concepts is a small group of management consultants in Los Angeles. The mark pictographically suggests "counseling" or "consultation" by the gesture of the figure on the right. I feel that the mark clearly and immediately communicates the essential idea out of a quite abstract and complex work category. It is always used in black and white.

Designer: Harry Murphy & Friends
San Francisco, California

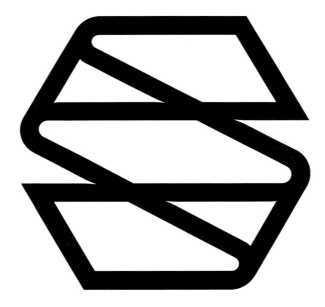

Sierracin Corporation, a producer of plastic laminates for auto and aerospace windows. This mark was inspired by the designer's bending of a strip of clear acetate into an "S" shape. Although that looked very little like the end result, it provided the right direction to follow.

Designer: Carl Seltzer
Advertising Designers, Inc.
Los Angeles, California

Spectra-Physics, Inc., the world's leading laser manufacturer, began operations in 1963. Based on the principle of laser technology, this symbol, derived from the letterform "S," implies both energy and growth.

Designer: G. Dean Smith
San Francisco, California

The Storkline Furniture symbol was first used as a hang tag on all of the company products which were children's furniture only. The egg was used both positive and negative and the symbolic stork within was reversed as needed. The mark was also applied to all packaging and general graphics.

Designer: Goldsholl Associates
Northfield, Illinois

"The Summit" is a highrise condominium at the summit of Russian Hill in San Francisco. The building sits atop the very peak of Russian Hill, and its living spaces enjoy correspondingly magnificent views. The mark derives its meaning from a visual pun, in which the letterforms of the word "Summit" parody the conceptual idea of the project location and name.

Designer: Harry Murphy & Friends
San Francisco, California

Superior Metalworking Systems, Inc. is a company that deals in hydraulic self-centering steady rests, which clamp and support components to be machined, turned, drilled, bored, etc.

The "S" is made up of clamp-like hands grasping a component ready to be machined.

Designer: Bob Mendoza
            Los Angeles, California

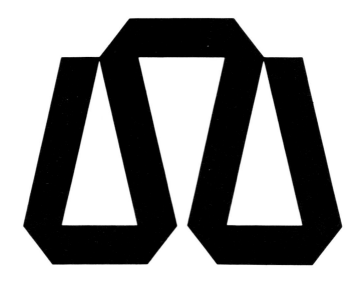

Located in San Francisco, the financial capital of the West, the firm of Sutro & Co. Incorporated is the West's oldest investment brokerage and has been represented from its inception by the balanced assayer's scales. When the company was incorporated in 1969, the original antique etching version of the symbol was updated to this far more contemporary and functional yet timeless mark.

Designer: G. Dean Smith
San Francisco, California

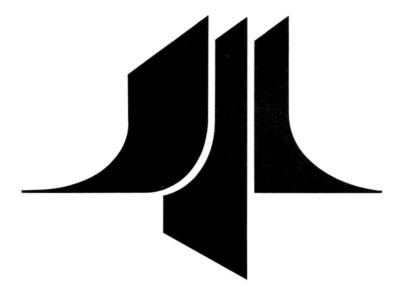

The Synthane-Taylor Corporation symbol evolved from merging the letters S and T, the first letters of the two companies that combined to form one. The design also symbolizes the lamination process.

Designer: Corporate Identities Division
Gray & Rogers, Inc.
Philadelphia, Pennsylvania

Technicolor

This is an example of a logotype trademark — there is no symbol. Consequently, it was necessary to create an alphabet unique to the mark. The trouble with this approach to logotype alphabets is that the more unique it becomes the more illegible it usually becomes. We do not believe this to be the case in the Technicolor logotype.

One very bothersome problem with a long name like Technicolor is that with most rounded letters the word is too extended to be practical. This is particularly true with all capital letters. Yet attempts to overcome this problem with condensed letters produced other aesthetic problems — they looked lousy.

The particular solution is this case was to chop the sides of rounded letters. This conserved space without the effect of a condensed letter. It also resulted in an unique but highly readable logotype. Don't you agree?

Designer: Robert Miles Runyan & Associates
Los Angeles, California

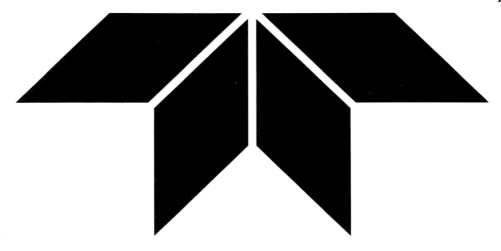

Perhaps the most important element we strive for in creating a corporate symbol is that of motion. The dynamics of motion in a symbol does two things. One, it attracts the eye, and two, there seems to be some relationship with motion dynamics and memorability.

Although it is not necessary to incorporate the initials of the corporate name in the company's symbol, it is a good starting place. And frequently, as in the case of the Teledyne mark, it works so well that further exploration only brings you back to the same point.

Teledyne is a high-technology organization with many diversified divisions. Their symbol we feel shows the parts working to create the whole initial "T," certainly symbolic of the way the company is structured. At the same time, there is a sweeping thrust upward created by the juncture of white space between the diamond shaped parts of the composite initial "T."

Designer: Robert Miles Runyan & Associates
Los Angeles, California

TERADYNE

Logo for a manufacturer of automatic testing equipment — Teradyne. The company wished to emphasize their name rather than a symbolic approach because they plan to become involved in many product areas and do not want the logo to become inappropriate in the future.

Designer: Dave Lizotte
Gunn Associates
Boston, Massachusetts

Texas Real Estate News masthead. This masthead appears in green on newsprint paper. In this instance, our aim was to upgrade outdated newspaper tabloids of this nature with a contemporary approach. We wanted to incorporate Texas, the Lone Star state, into the total statement and still keep our simplicity and quick identity.

Designer: Don Day
                  Unigraphics, Inc.
                  Dallas, Texas

The central Sierra Nevada range of California is the location of Timberwine, a year-round community that in 1973 was master-planned to exist in harmony with its environment. Surrounded by National Forest, Timberwine is the only community of its kind in its geographical setting and in its multiplicity of planned facilities and activities. The highly timbered mountainous area is suggested in the form of the symbol, with the series of stirations reflecting the various functions of schools, shopping centers, recreation areas and residences.

Designer: G. Dean Smith
San Francisco, California

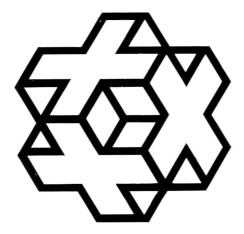

Total Financial Services is an investment counseling service. The mark was developed to suggest the multiplicity of investing and building assets. Based on the plus (+) sign and multiplication symbol, although not actually either, and combined to suggest a structure or framework of growth.

Designer: Gerry Rosentswieg
The Graphics Studio
Los Angeles, California

130

USEMCO Inc. is a small manufacturer of water and sewage lift stations marketed primarily to municipalities. A more modern and organized identity program was deemed essential to support a broadened sales effort in the municipal market and an introductory program aimed at industry. The new trademark was designed to convey the industrial strength of USEMCO's products and the feeling of movement associated with their function.

Designer: William Cagney
RVI Corporation
Chicago, Illinois

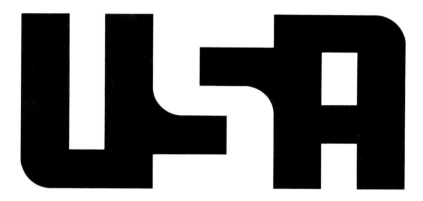

USA — a proposed mark for the government of the United States. Color is vital to this mark, and therefore considered a primary element. The "U" is red, the "A" is blue, and of course the negative space between them, which forms the "S," is white when used on a white field.

The negative "S" is seen secondarily, but once it is recognized, it becomes an asset because it exists through the viewer's visual participation.

Designer: Carl Seltzer
Advertising Designers, Inc.
Los Angeles, California

132

This mark was designed for a U.S.I.A. exhibit, "Research and Development USA" scheduled to tour Russia in 1971 and 1972. Subsequently it went through most of the Eastern zone countries. This flag solution was set up in red, white and blue and it was derived from the forms of a printed circuit.

Designer: George Nelson & Company
                    New York, N.Y.

This USA symbol was also done for the U.S.I.A. exhibit, "Research and Development USA." It was done with light directly on sensitive paper, the idea again being to reflect the technological theme.

Designer: George Nelson & Company
New York, N.Y.

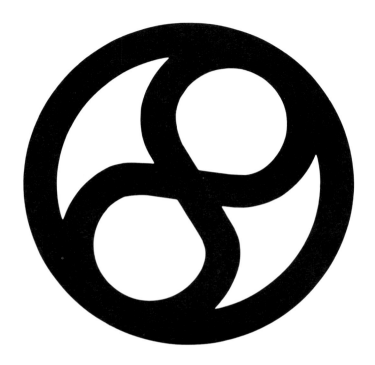

The major United States corporation in the field of recycling systems and hardware components is the parent corporation of Unifinity Foundation, established in 1974. The foundation is operated on the premise of returning a portion of its parent company's profits to research and conservation for the betterment of mankind. The symbol of Unifinity Foundation is based on the idea of a continuum, both of nature's resources and of human effort, expressed through the scientific sign of infinity.

Designer: G. Dean Smith
San Francisco, California

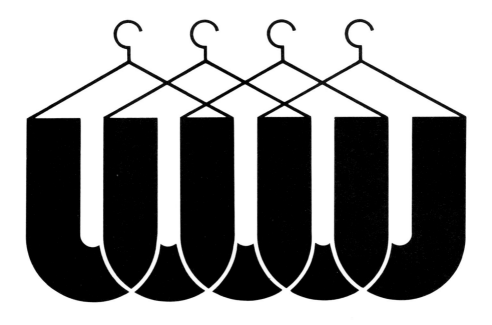

Uniforms Unlimited, Inc. specializes in industrial and medical uniforms with a chain of retail stores located throughout Southern California.

Their corporate logo suggests both the name of the firm and the nature of its business by a series of uniform, overlapping U's suspended from clothes hangers. It is used in its pure black form for store, garment label, advertisement and business form identification. Stationery use involves blind embossing on canary yellow paper with hangers and discrete type printed in black.

Designer: Thomas A. Rigsby
TriArts, Inc.
Los Angeles, California

The United Engineers symbol evolved from the hook that is synonomous with construction equipment. The "e" from "Engineers" is incorporated in the sytlized hook.

Designer: Corporate Identities Division
Gray & Rogers, Inc.
Philadelphia, Pennsylvania

Vaughn Walls, Inc., a company that designs and installs movable and fixed wall partitions in commercial and industrial buildings. The company produces a product line of very fine quality and craftsmanship. This was an important consideration in developing their corporate program. The symbol was deisgned as a plumb bob, a device used in the building to check whether a wall is vertical. The inner portion of the symbol is the actual blumb bob set into a "V" for Vaughn Walls.

Designer: Dennis S. Juett
            Los Angeles, California

Vantage Planning Systems completes working drawings (construction) for its parent company, the Vantage Companies.

Since they are involved with topographic studies of land and their blueprints are characterized by a multitude of lines, the development of this symbol to reflect the characteristics of their work was only natural.

Designer: Jack Evans
Unigraphics, Inc.
Dallas, Texas

"The Vault" is a franchised line of personal storage warehouses appealing to the young apartment dweller in urban and the large suburban areas, as well as the small businessman who needs temporary additional storage space. The buildings are distinctive in color and design and the image will be reinforced by newspaper and promotional exposure.

Designer: Adrianne Gregory
The Design Partnership/Bruce Beck Associates
Evanston, Illinois

Vista was a magazine of the United Nations and international affairs. Its outlook was unpartisan, its policy to both sides of an issue in a search for truth and understanding.

The logotype with its property of reading right-side-up or up-side-down is a somewhat esoteric expression of the two sidedness of debate. The distortion of the letter forms lends an appropriate character of internationality. The actual mechanics of this solution are somewhat mysterious to me. How or why I recognized that this five-letter word could be molded into a right-reading inversion has always remained unclear to me. But it was the immediate solution and no other exploration was tried. I was blessed with a receptive and perceptive editor and Vista had a distinctive masthead in a matter of hours.

Designer: Richard Hess Inc.
New York City

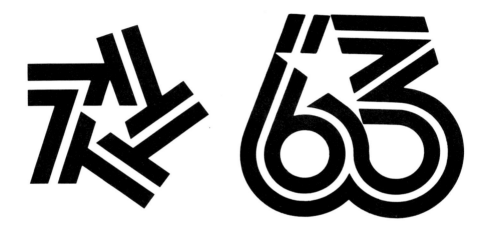

WMAL, Channel 7 in Washington, D. C., is the major owned television broadcasting facility of Washington Star Communications, Inc. Contained in the symbol, designed in 1969, is the numeral "7" which multiplies and radiates to form the shape of a star.

The parent corporation star has also been applied to the WMAL Radio 63 symbol which denotes the station's position on the radio dial.

Designer: G. Dean Smith
San Francisco, California

142

Western Mutual Insurance Company offers security to homeowners by specializing in fire and theft policies. The company is represented by agencies in the western states.

Using two key words, security and residential, as a trade mark basis, oblique planes are brought into close proximities to suggest rooftops and mutual security. At the same time, the letters W and M are formed with the W slightly to the west of the M, further emphasizing the company.

When adapted to color, reddish brown is used for the W for earthiness, and black is used for the M for conservatism.

Designer: Thomas A. Rigsby
T. Rigsby, Design
West Los Angeles, California

Western Ventures, a real estate development company based in Los Angeles, specializes in multiple dwellings: condominiums, apartment complexes, etc.

This logo tries to emphasize the free spirit of living in the California southland. The initials "W" and "V" are suggested by the birds in flight.

The birds also convey the feelings of freedom of spirit and lifestyle. Horizontal lines form the strong land symbol. The logo is printed in light blue to further the light, free feeling.

Designer: Bob Mendoza
             Los Angeles, California

Westlake Moving & Storage System, a moving and storage company serving the Southern California area. The company was formed in 1908 and has maintained a very personal and close family relationship between management, employees and clients throughout its continuous growth and prosperity.

The symbol was designed to take on the quality of a toy truck to carry through the family, personal feeling, although in reality Westlake has been a pioneer and leader in moving delicate sophisticated electronic equipment, office and residential furnishings. The symbol combines a "W" for the van portion of the truck and a simple shaped cab and wheels. When used in color, the "W" prints the second color and the truck cab and wheels remain black.

Designer: Dennis S. Juett
Los Angeles, California

White Birch Lakes

White Birch Lakes, vacation homesites in Michigan. This is depicted by using a strong styilzation of white birch trees, which are natural to the area, combined with the water from the lakes.

Designer: Corporate Identities Division
Gray & Rogers, Inc.
Philadelphia, Pennsylvania

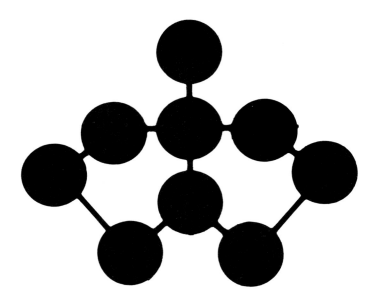

Creative and highly specialized artistic construction is the unique talent of Wingers Erection Company. Designed in 1974, the symbol is based on natural forms of construction, such as the triangle used which through repetition has been expanded to form the letter "W." Because of the nature of its business, Wingers Erection Company travels from place to place, and this idea has been suggested by the form of Gerria Remigis.

Designer: G. Dean Smith
San Francisco, California

Yosemite National Park is an area comprising 1,200 square miles. Yet the single most spectacular, visited, known and recognized world-wide landmark within the park is the glacier-carved, sheer granite face of Half Dome. Though Yosemite is many things to many people, the pictogram of Half Dome, designed in 1965, was without question the ideal singular presentation of the park for visitors both national and international.

Designer: G. Dean Smith
            San Francisco, California

The Young Musicians Foundation is the sponsor of the Los Angeles Junior Philharmonic and the donors of study grants for young musicians. The symbol is based on the clef signatures, denoting music. The profile was incorporated to imply a personification or humanism.

The symbol in total depicts youthful music makers.

Designer: Gerry Rosentswieg
The Graphics Studio
Los Angeles, California

Designers

Advertising Designers, Inc., 818 N. LaBrea Avenue, Los Angeles, California 90038

Primo Angeli, 350 Pacific, San Francisco, California 94111

Appelbaum & Curtis Inc., 333 East 49th, New York, N.Y. 10017

Bruce Beck Design Associates Inc., Fountain Square Building, 1601 Sherman Avenue, Evanston Illinois 60201

Dickens Design Group, 13 West Grand Avenue, Chicago, Illinois 60610

Goldsholl Associates, 420 Frontage Road, Northfield, Illinois 60093

The Graphics Studio, 8721 Beverly Boulevard, Los Angeles, California 90048

Gray & Rogers, Corporate Identity Division, 1234 Market Street, Philadelphia, Pennsylvania 19107

Gunn Associates, 275 Newbury Street, Boston, Massachusetts 02116

Richard Hess Inc., 217 E. 49th Street, New York, N.Y. 10017

Dennis S. Juett & Associates, 672 South Lafayette Park Place, Los Angeles, California 90057

Kramer, Miller, Lomden, Glassman, 1528 Waverly Street, Philadelphia, Pennsylvania 19146

Walter Landor Associates, Ferryboat Klamath, Pier 5, San Francisco, California 94111

Lippincott & Margulies, Inc., 277 Park Avenue New York, N.Y. 10017

Charles MacMurray Design Inc., 233 E. Ontario Street, Chicago, Illinois 60611

Bob Mendoza, 1266 Lilac Terrace, Los Angeles, California 90026

Miller/Hernandez Design Consultants, 90 W. Wieuca Road, N.E., Atlanta, Georgia 30342

Harry Murphy & Friends, 950 Columbus, San Francisco, California

George Nelson & Company, 251
Park Avenue South, New York,
N.Y. 10010

Robert Pease & Company, 1636
Bush Street, San Francisco,
California 94109

Mel Richman Inc., 15 North
Presidential Boulevard, Bala-Cynwyd,
Pennsylvania 19004

T. Rigsby Design, 1015 N. Fairfax
Avenue, Los Angeles, California
90046

Robert Miles Runyan & Associates,
1801 Avenue of the Stars, Los
Angeles, California 90067

RVI Corporation, One IBM Plaza,
Chicago, Illinois 60611

G. Dean Smith, 633 Battery Street,
San Francisco, California

Tri-Arts, Inc., 1015 N. Fairfax
Avenue, Los Angeles, California 90046

Unigraphics, Inc., 2525 Stemmons
Expressway, Suite 955, Dallas,
Texas 75207